Living in Light, Love, Peace, and Abundance

Living in Light, Love, Peace, and Abundance

By KK Smith

This book is a collection of inspirational quotes by the author, Kenya (KK) Smith, as well as images and quotes by other noted authors.

©2015, Kenya (KK) Smith. All rights reserved. Except as permitted by the U.S. Copyright Act of 1976, no part of this publication may be reproduced, distributed, or transmitted in any form or by any means, or stored in a database or retrieval system, without the prior written permission of the publisher, excepting brief quotes and in reviews.

Portions of this book contain quotes and images from others authors that are noted, as well as, quotes that are unknown.

Printed in the United States of America

Dedicated to my Black Beautiful Flower & YOU!

The journey of this book started with me looking for inspiration for myself to do and be better. When I saw the wealth of inspiration, I thought of how it could possibly help many others. We are all connected by one simple need and that is LOVE! We all need pure love from ourselves and to give to others.

With this book I hope to inspire, uplift, and bring peace and joy to others.

On my journey for inspiration I found countless of motivational quotes on social media sites. I also began to write some of my own quotes during the process.

The majority of these quotes and images are by other artists that are noted with their information. Please go to their pages to find more amazing quotes and images.

May you have abundant Love and Peace!!

Living in Light, Love, Peace, and Abundance

Life	pg. 1
Goals	pg. 22
Friendships & Relationships	pg. 44
Spirituality	pg. 66
You	pg. 92

Quotes & Images
Credits

Life

Image: @Nativeparty	pg. 1
Bible	pg. 2
KK Smith: Quote/Image: Big Stock download	pg. 3
Think Grow Prosper @thinkgrowprosper	pg. 4
Quote & Image: KK Smith	pg. 5
Unknown	pg. 6
@sarattaspeaks www.sarattaspeaks.com	pg. 7
KK Smith: Quote/ Image: Big Stock download	pg. 8
Unknown	pg. 9
Maya Angelou	pg. 10
KK Smith: Quote/ Image: Big Stock download	pg. 11
Unknown	pg. 12
Image & Quote: KK Smith	pg. 13
Unknown	pg. 14
Unknown	pg. 15
@singleorginquotes	pg. 16
KK Smith: Quote/ Image: Big Stock download	pg. 17
Unknown	pg. 18
Iyanla Vanzant/Image: Big Stock download	pg. 19
Unknown	pg. 20
KK Smith: Quote/ Image: Suzanne Toon	pg. 21

Goals

Image: @Rose_illes	pg. 23
Bible	pg. 24
KK Smith: Image & Quote	pg. 25
Oprah: Quote/Image: Big Stock download	pg. 26
@singleorginquotes	pg. 27
KK Smith: Quote/Image: Big Stock download	pg. 28
Unknown	pg. 29
KK Smith: Quote & Image	pg. 30
Unknown	pg. 31
Steve Martin & KK Smith	pg. 32
Bishop T.D. Jakes: Quotes/Image: KK Smith	pg. 33
Carrie Green	pg. 34
KK Smith: Quote & Image	pg. 35
Think Grow Prosper @thinkgrowprosper	pg. 36
Quote #1: Unknown/Quote #2: KK Smith	pg. 37
@roller_coaster_of_life	pg. 38
KK Smith	pg. 39
Sherita Leslie: Quote www.sheritaleslie.com/Image:KK Smith	pg. 40
Chanique Stewart	pg. 41
KK Smith: Quote/Image:Vecteezy	pg. 42

Friends and Relationships

Image: Big Stock download	pg. 44
Bible	pg. 45
KK Smith: Quote/Image: Huffington Post	pg. 46
Unknown	pg. 47
Unknown	pg. 48
KK Smith: Quote/Image: Big Stock download	pg. 49
Think Grow Prosper	pg. 50
Unknown	pg. 51
Quote #1: Unknown/Quote #2: KK Smith	pg. 52
Chanique Stewart	pg. 53
KK Smith: Quote/Image: Big Stock download	pg. 54
Unknown	pg. 55
Nina Simone	pg. 56
KK Smith: Quote/ Image: Pinterest (Unknown)	pg. 57
@roller_coaster_of_life	pg. 58
KK Smith: Image and Quote	pg. 59
@thisspirituallife	pg. 60
KK Smith	pg. 61
Melinda Gates	pg. 62
Sigmund Freud	pg. 63
Bible/Image: Big Stock download	pg. 64

Spirituality

Image: Vecteezy	pg. 66
Bible	pg. 67
Image: Vecteezy	pg. 68
Image: Big Stock download	pg. 69
Image Big Stock download	pg. 70
KK Smith	pg. 71
Think Grow Prosper	pg. 72
Quote #1: Unknown/Quote #2: KK Smith	pg. 73
Chanique Stewart	pg. 74
Mary Engelbrit/Rebecca Halton	pg. 75
Unknown/Bible	pg. 76
Unknown/ KK Smith	pg. 77
Joseph Campbell/Bible	pg. 78
AJ Johnson @theajzone	pg. 79
@instagodministries	pg. 80
Unknown/Bible	pg. 81
Unknown/Bible	pg. 82
@seruh.solo	pg. 83
Unknown	pg. 84
Unknown	pg. 85
Unknown	pg. 86
@singleorginquotes	pg. 87
@Jwarhol	pg. 88
Bible: Quote/Image: Unknown	pg. 89
Joan of Arc	pg. 90

You
Meryl @meryl_tm	pg. 92
Bible	pg. 93
Kenya Smith: Quote/ Image: Vecteezy	pg. 94
Unknown	pg. 95
Unknown	pg. 96
Think Grow Prosper @thinkgrowprosper	pg. 97
Quote #1: Mandy Hale/ Quote #2: @ninablogwriter	pg. 98
Chanique Stewart	pg. 99
KK Smith: Quote/Image: Big Stock download	pg. 100
Unknown	pg. 101
Unknown	pg. 102
@shedavi_	pg. 103
Unknown	pg. 104
AJ Johnson @theajzone	pg. 105
@bodypopactive	pg. 106
KK Smith	pg. 107
Unknown	pg. 108
Quote #1: Unknown/Quote #2: KK Smith	pg. 109
Quote #1: Unknown/Quote #2: Bible	pg. 110
Quote #1:Unknown/Quote #2: KK Smith	pg. 111
Mark Nepo: Quote/Image: Vecteezy	pg. 112
Maya Angelo	pg. 113
Quote #1: Unknown/Quote #2: KK Smith	pg. 114
@be.here.now	pg. 115
Rebecca Halton www.RebeccaHalton.com	pg. 116
Marieanne Williamson	pg. 117

Life

"With you is the source of life. By your light we can see light." _ Psalms 36:9

"Live in light. Travel Light. Spread the light. Be the LIGHT!"
– KK Smith

"Always speak the truth the 1st time and you won't be asked asked a 2nd time." – KK Smith

THERE WILL BE MANY CHAPTERS IN YOUR LIFE. DON'T GET LOST IN THE ONE YOU'RE IN NOW

Never sacrifice these three things: your family, your heart, or your dignity.

"Eat for the right reasons!

Eat for health. Eat for beauty. Eat to live!" – KK Smith

"Always be kinder than you feel."

— Unknown

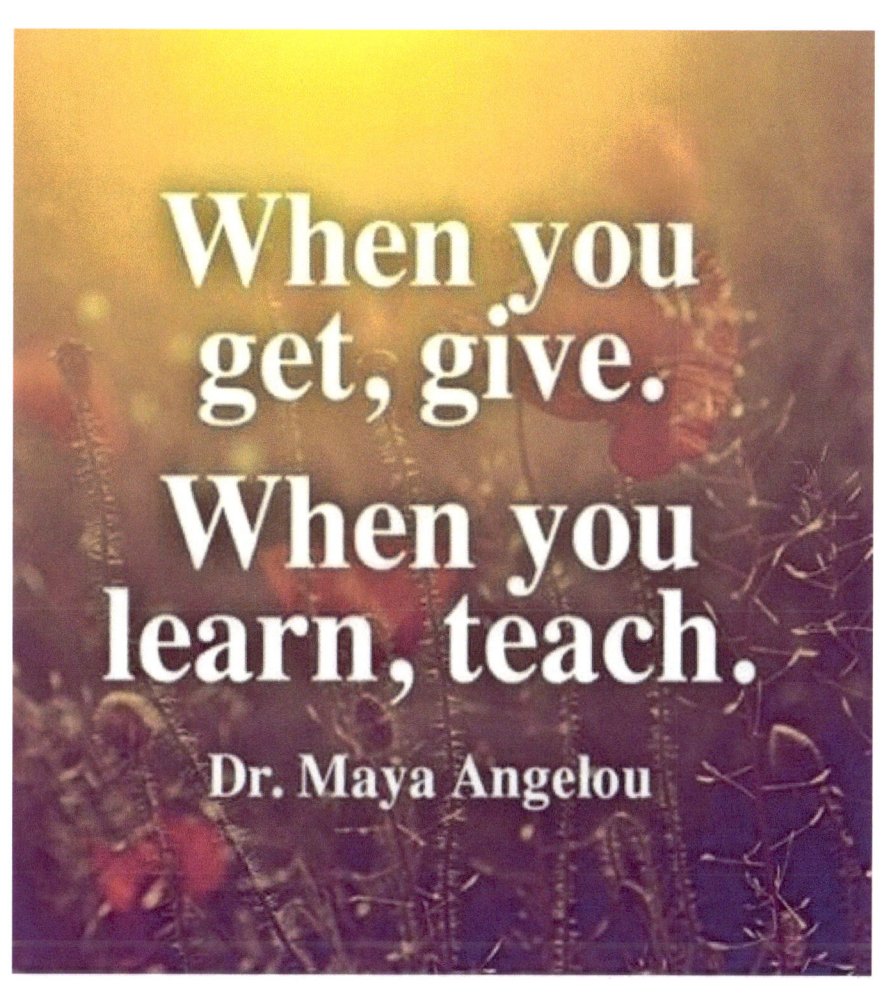

"Trying to always conquer the world can sometimes run you ragged. It can leave no room for valued time for you or anyone else in your life! Some days the greatest move you should conquer is to quiet your mind and be STILL." -

KK Smith

WORK FOR A CAUSE, **NOT** *FOR APPLAUSE. LIVE LIFE TO EXPRESS,* **NOT** *TO IMPRESS. DON'T STRIVE TO MAKE YOUR PRESENCE NOTICED, JUST MAKE YOUR ABSENCE FELT*

-Unknown

"Live life like a child. Live with wonderment and curiosity! Look for the beauty in everything and you will live a joyous life!!" – KK Smith

"Life is an echo. What you send out, comes back. What you sow, you reap. What you give, you get. What you see in others, exists in you. Remember, life is an echo. It always gets back to you. So give goodness."

—Unknown

"A change happened effortlessly the second you took a breath. Change is as simple or complicated as YOU make it!" – KK Smith

Sometimes Life is
About Risking
Everything For
A Dream No One
Can See But YOU!

-unknown

"There will be good days and bad days and we should be grateful for them all. Each day is a blessing and what you do with your blessings determines how you will be blessed!" – Iyanla Vanzant *do the right thing even when the wrong thing is happening*

"I went outside, with no phone and no music…I saw creation and I appreciated Life!"
– KK Smith

Goals

"Indeed, just as the body without spirit is dead, so also faith without works is dead." - James 2:26

"Use your own light to SHINE. You don't know how long it'll be when someone else's will dim."

- KK Smith

God doesn't need approval from your friends or family to make your vision come true.

"People think you're crazy when you don't do what they want you to do... Then people will think you're brilliant when you succeed at what they'll never do." – KK Smith

Remember how you dreamed, before you were told you couldn't.

Remember your goals, before you made mistakes.

Remember your ideas, before they didn't happen.

Remember your faith, now may it be restored.

Amen

-unknown

"Be so good at what you do that people google you."-

KK Smith

"You can't explain to a turtle a giraffe decision." – Bishop T.D. Jakes

SHE KNEW
THE POWER OF
HER MIND
& *so*
PROGRAMMED IT
for SUCCESS.

[CARRIE GREEN]

"I want to be a trained ballerina...

Learn how to be a ballerina.

Practice being a ballerina.

Be a trained ballerina.

Learn. Practice. BE."

-KK Smith

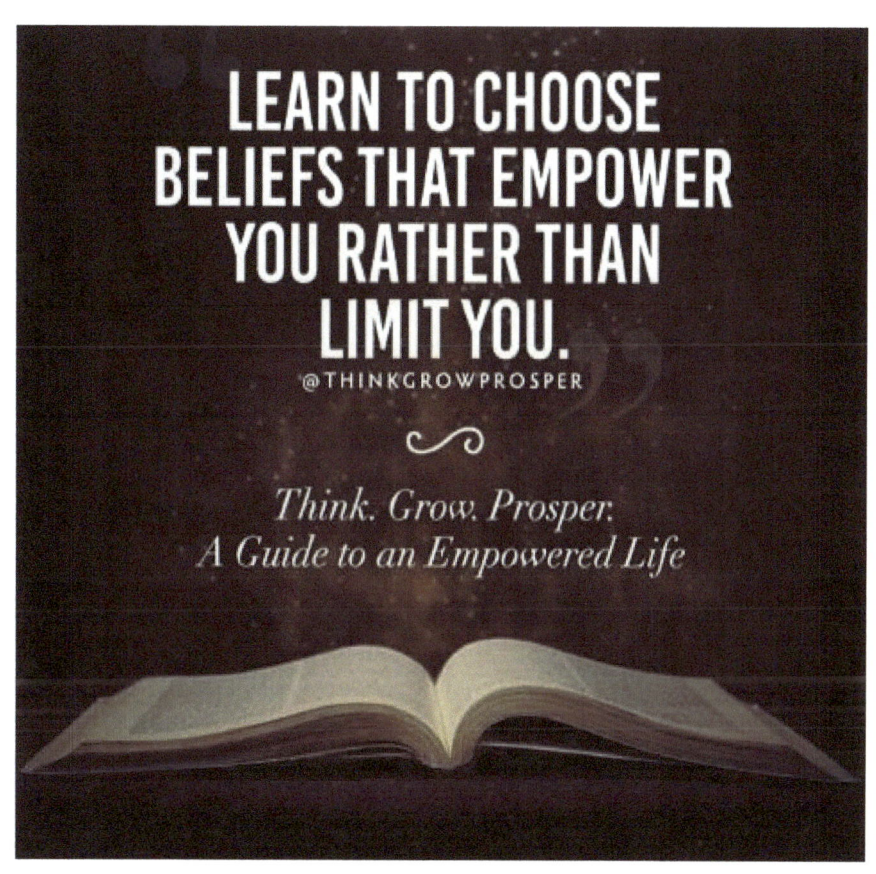

You did not wake up today to be mediocre

"God woke you up today for a purpose. Be the greatest YOU, to live in your purpose!!" – KK Smith

Don't limit your challenges, challenge your limits!

@roller_coaster_of_life

"A DREAM WITHOUT ACTION IS A NIGHTMARE! TAKE THE ACTION TO MAKE YOUR DREAM A REALITY."- KK Smith

"Everyday choose to look fear in the face and walk confidently in the direction of your dreams. Every step kills doubt and every achievement makes the dream real."- Sherita Leslie

> "IT IS BETTER TO BE RESPECTED THAN TO BE RICH. A GOOD NAME IS WORTH MORE THAN SILVER OR GOLD."
> CHANIQUE STEWART

"Remember not to sell yourself short. Too many girls chasing paper and leaving their minds behind. Chase greatness, soak in wisdom, provide value, and money will chase you." – Chanique Stewart

TODAY!

"Smile Today. Help others Today. Laugh Today.

Work towards your goals Today. Love Today. Be grateful Today.

Rest and Repeat tomorrow." – KK Smith

Friends & Relationships

"The second is this, 'You must love your neighbor as yourself.' There is no other commandment greater than these." - Mark 12:31

"When you have abundant, true love, it's like having hot, Krispy Kreme doughnuts everyday!!" - KK Smith

Friendship isn't about who you've known the longest.
It's about who walked into your life,
said "I'm here for you" and proved it.

Lessons Learned In Life

"Find a mate that Truly loves GOD and you will have a mate that Truly loves you." – KK Smith

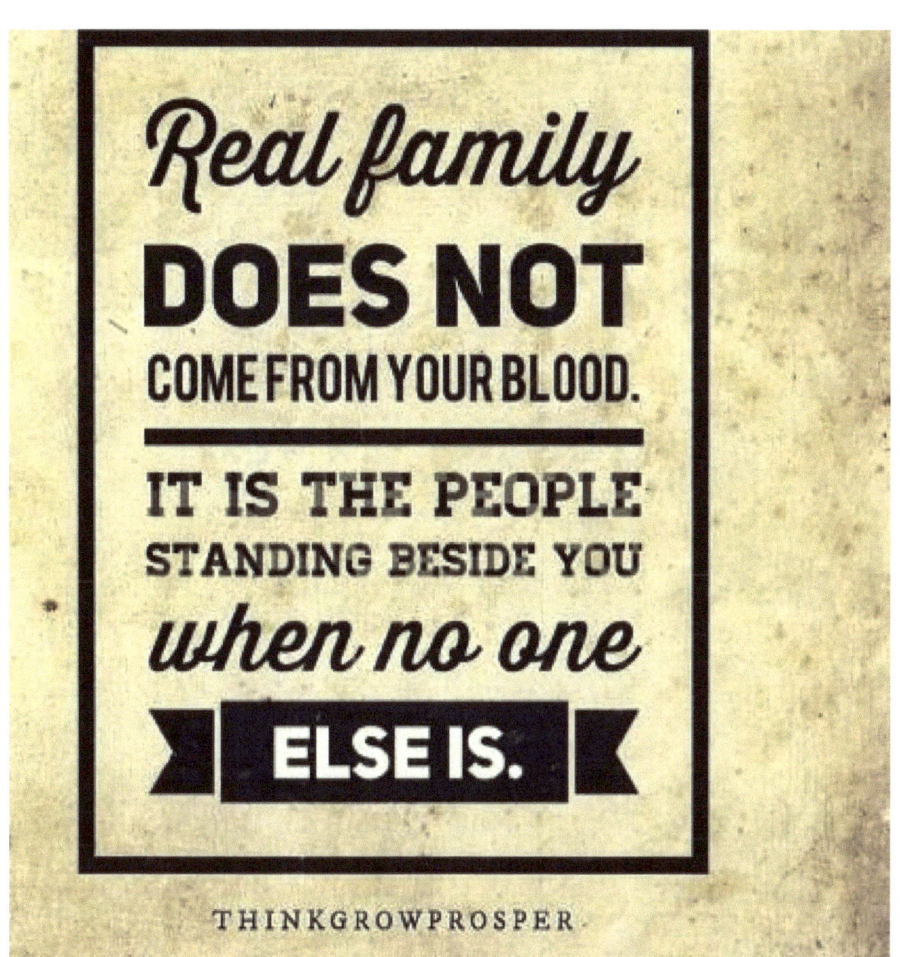

Characterize people by their actions and you will never be fooled by their words

"Don't go spiritually and mentally bankrupt investing your time in the wrong people." - KK Smith

"A REAL RELATIONSHIP IS NOT
BUILT ON BEING NICE;
IT'S BUILT ON BEING REAL."

CHANIQUE STEWART
Nailjam strange coach

Womenwithambition

JUST Because it's True, Doesn't mean it should be said!!

"With relationships & conversations, ask yourself, 'Is what I have to say upbuilding or tearing someone down? What is the REAL purpose of the conversation?' Be certain that if the circle you're with is negatively talking about someone else now, they're doing the same to you later. Use TRUTH Positively." – KK Smith

Love people
For who they are
And not for who
You want them
To be. That's
Where the
Disconnection
Starts.

"You have to learn to get up from the table when love is no longer being served." - Nina Simone

"Evaluate WHO you are on the inside to better understand & determine WHO you attract on the outside." – KK Smith

"When I compliment you, I compliment myself, because I am who I associate with!" - @roller_coaster_of_life

When you decide to Truly

LOVE

Yourself, you can only then be able to whole heatedly love others. Then prepare for the beautiful, abundance of love that will surround you!"

- KK Smith

SPEAK IN SUCH A WAY THAT OTHERS LOVE TO LISTEN TO YOU.

LISTEN IN SUCH A WAY THAT OTHERS LOVE TO SPEAK TO YOU.

One

"We are ONE. Life was breathe into you and I was made from you, so we are One. I am my own best friend, because you are my best friend, we are One. I follow you and you follow Christ with GOD as our head, through love we are united as ONE!" – KK Smith

Connect *deeply* with others. Our *humanity* is the only thing *we all have* in common.

MELINDA GATES

> "How bold one gets when one is sure of being loved."
>
> — Sigmund Freud

"Love is patient and kind. Love is not jealous. It does not brag, does not get puffed up, does not behave indecently, does not look for its own interests, does not become provoked. It does not keep account of the injury. It does not rejoice over unrighteousness, but rejoices with the truth. It bears all things, believes all things, hopes all things, endures all things." – 1 Corinthians 13:4-7

Spirituality

"*And now, my sons, listen to me. Yes, happy are those who keeps my ways. Listen to discipline and become wise, and never neglect it.*" – Proverbs 8:32-33

"Beauty was created. It was created good. In order for us to receive all the good that comes from the beauty that was created, it is up to us to appreciate and cherish it everyday." - *KK Smith*

"A rainy day. A failed relationship. A lost job. There is a time, reason, and season for everything. The blessing is always with you." – KK Smith

"Our circumstances and seasons don't decide our potential to BLOOM, right where we are. It's amazing what GOD can use to bring forth BEAUTY, if and when we let HIM." – Rebecca Halton

"We weren't created in mans' image, we were created in GOD'S image. Once you accept that you are extraordinarily made, you will see that you are not made to fit in with ordinary people." – KK Smith

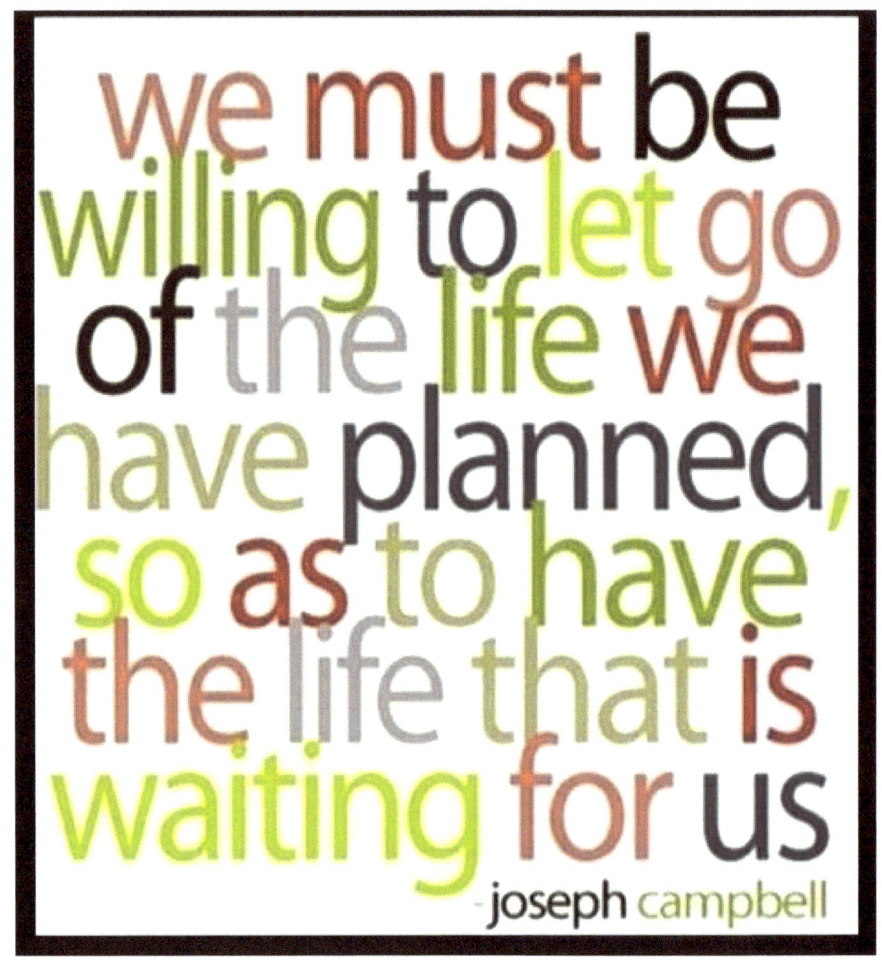

"The plans of the diligent surely lead to success, but all who are hasty, surely head for poverty."- Proverbs 21:5

God didn't place the limit on your greatness... You did

"Today's word- LIMITS! DECIDE to remove them! That's the hardest part...DECIDING that you are worthy, deserving, capable? But oooweee...Once you make that decision your choices begin to reflect the brighter light within you!! My dad taught me that "NO" simply means 'not now' or 'not this way'...Today decide to erase, delete, remove, let go of the limits to the great you can be and let GOD take you to levels you can't even imagine!! GO!" – AJ

TRUST IN GOD'S TIMING. IT'S BETTER TO WAIT A WHILE AND HAVE THINGS FALL INTO PLACE THAN TO RUSH AND HAVE THINGS FALL APART.
-@INSTAGODMINISTRIES

"I am with you always." - Matthew 28:20

> WHEN A COUPLE HAS WORSHIP TOGETHER, THEY NOT ONLY BECOME CLOSER TO GOD BUT CLOSER TO EACH OTHER

"Enjoy life with your beloved wife all the days of your futile life, which HE has given you under the sun." ~ Ecclesiastes 9:9

"And if not, HE is still GOOD!"-
@seruh.solo

Don't think of the things you didn't get after *praying.* Think of the **countless blessings** God gave you without *asking.*

WITHOUT DREAMS
WE REACH NOTHING.
WITHOUT LOVE
WE FEEL NOTHING.
WITHOUT GOD
WE ARE NOTHING.

Act, and God will act.

-- Joan of Arc

YOU

"I praise you because in an aweinspiring way I am wonderfully made. Your works are wonderful, I know this very well." - Psalms 139:14

New Season. New You. New Views. New Life. - KK Smith

YOU WERE STRONG ENOUGH TO GET THIS FAR.
YOU ARE STRONG ENOUGH TO KEEP GOING.

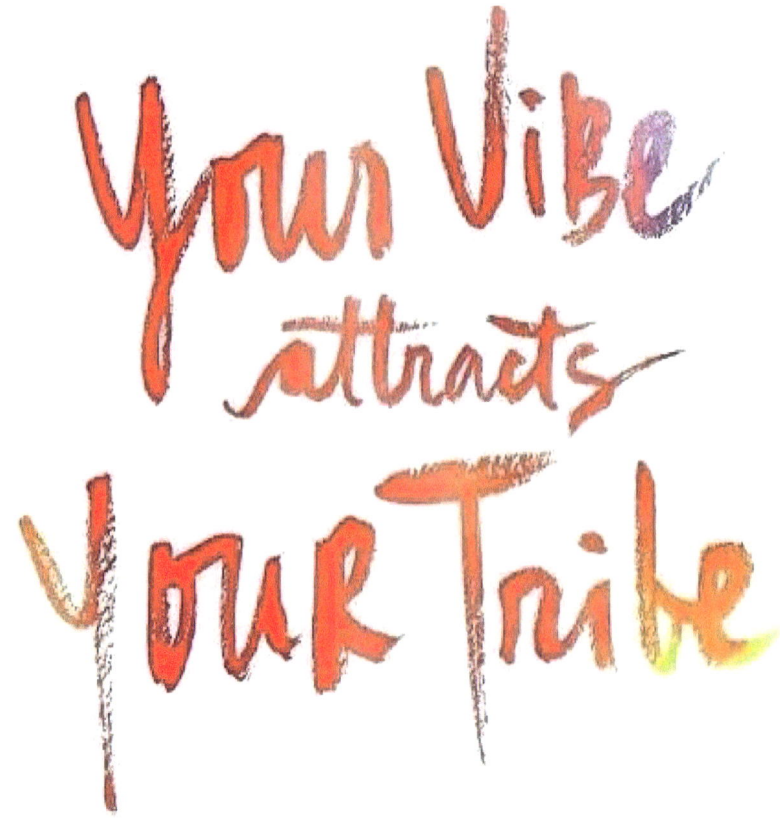

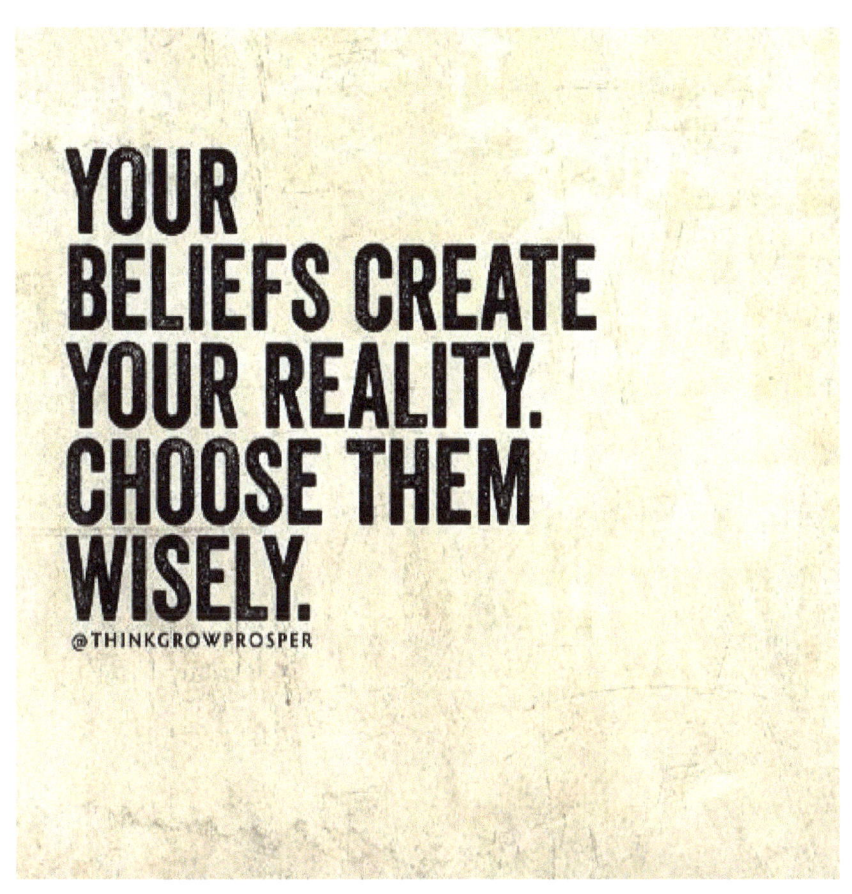

"No one can ever change you except yourself. So start your day with the greatest hope and never say NO before doing something." - @Nisablogwriter

"YOU WERE CREATED BY THE GREATEST EXPRESSION OF LOVE. LIVE IT!!"- KK SMITH

You've always been **beautiful.** Now you're just deciding to be healthier, fitter, faster & stronger. Remember that.

Nobody can take away your pain... so don't let anyone take away your happiness.

Live your life so clear it needs no explanation.

"Sometimes we caught up in our busy lives worrying about everyone else and forget to take care of ourselves. It's great to give other people your time because you care, but every once in awhile you have to take 'me time' and just relax"- @bodypopactive

Because

"Don't allow someone else's life determine your life...

No matter who wronged you. No matter who was/wasn't there for you/

No matter what you saw in your life.

You are accountable for YOU. Always choose the best,

Not Because." – KK Smith

You don't need someone to complete you. You only need someone to accept you *completely.*

You Can't Fix Yourself By Breaking Someone Else

"Breaking someone else down is only a reflection of how broken you are." – KK Smith

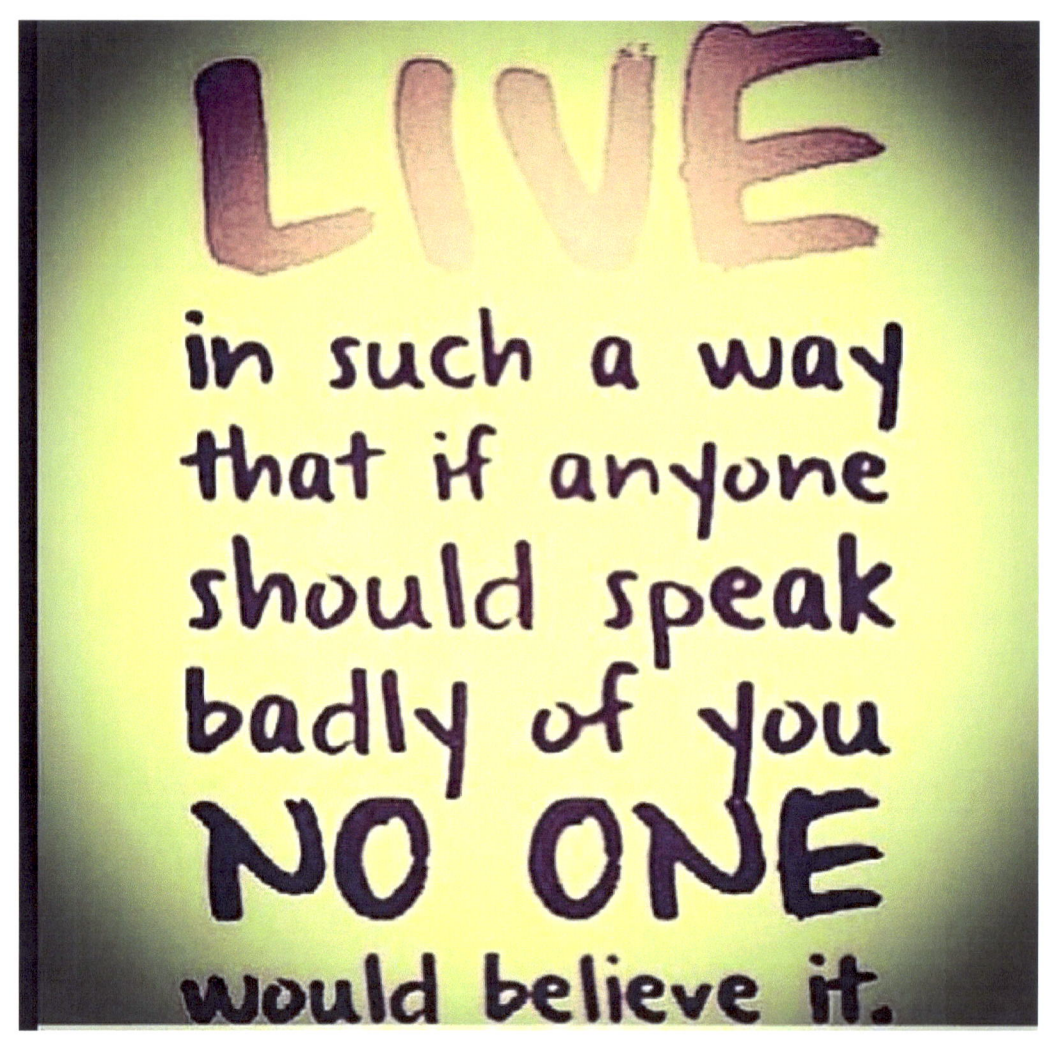

"So that you may make sure of the more important things, so that you may be flawless and not stumbling others." – Philippians 1:18

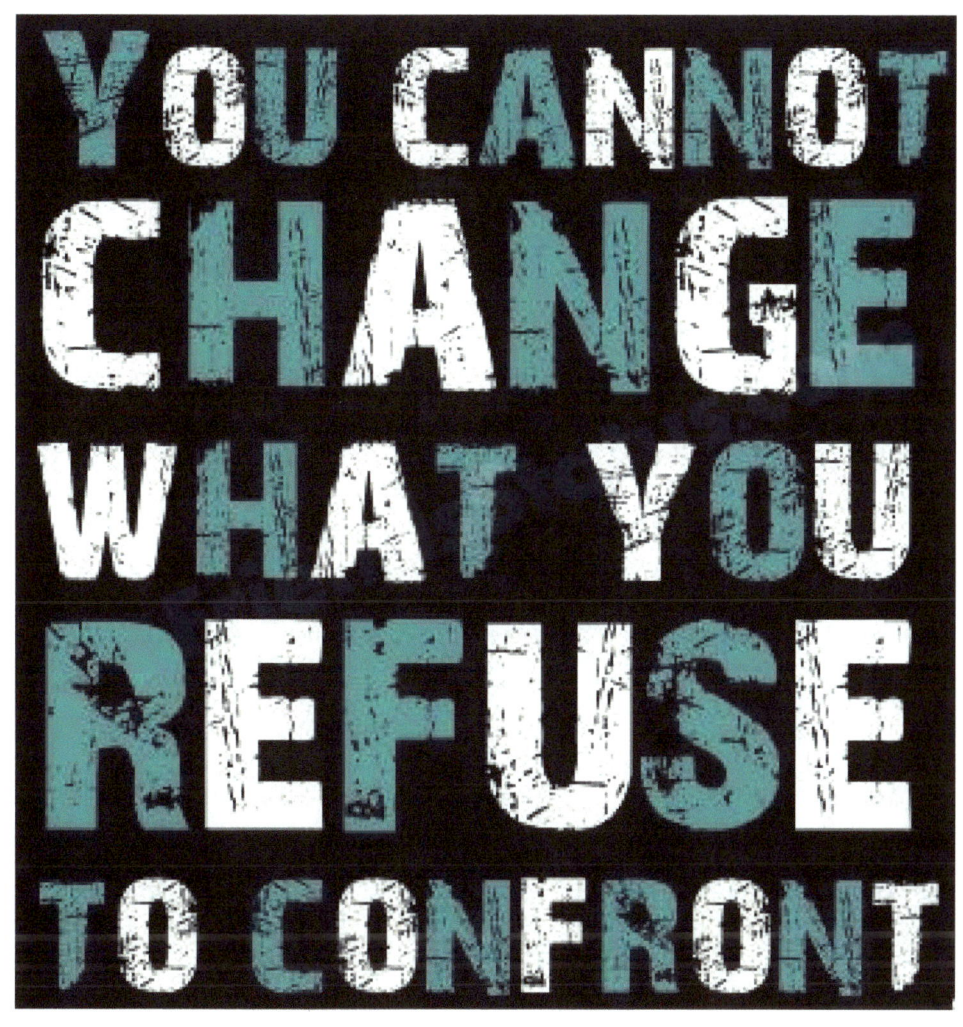

"Change doesn't come overnight. Neither does change come from doing NOTHING!" - KK Smith

"The longest journey you will make in your life is from your Head to your Heart."- Mark Nepo

Do the best you can until you know better. Then when you know better, do better.

– Maya Angelou

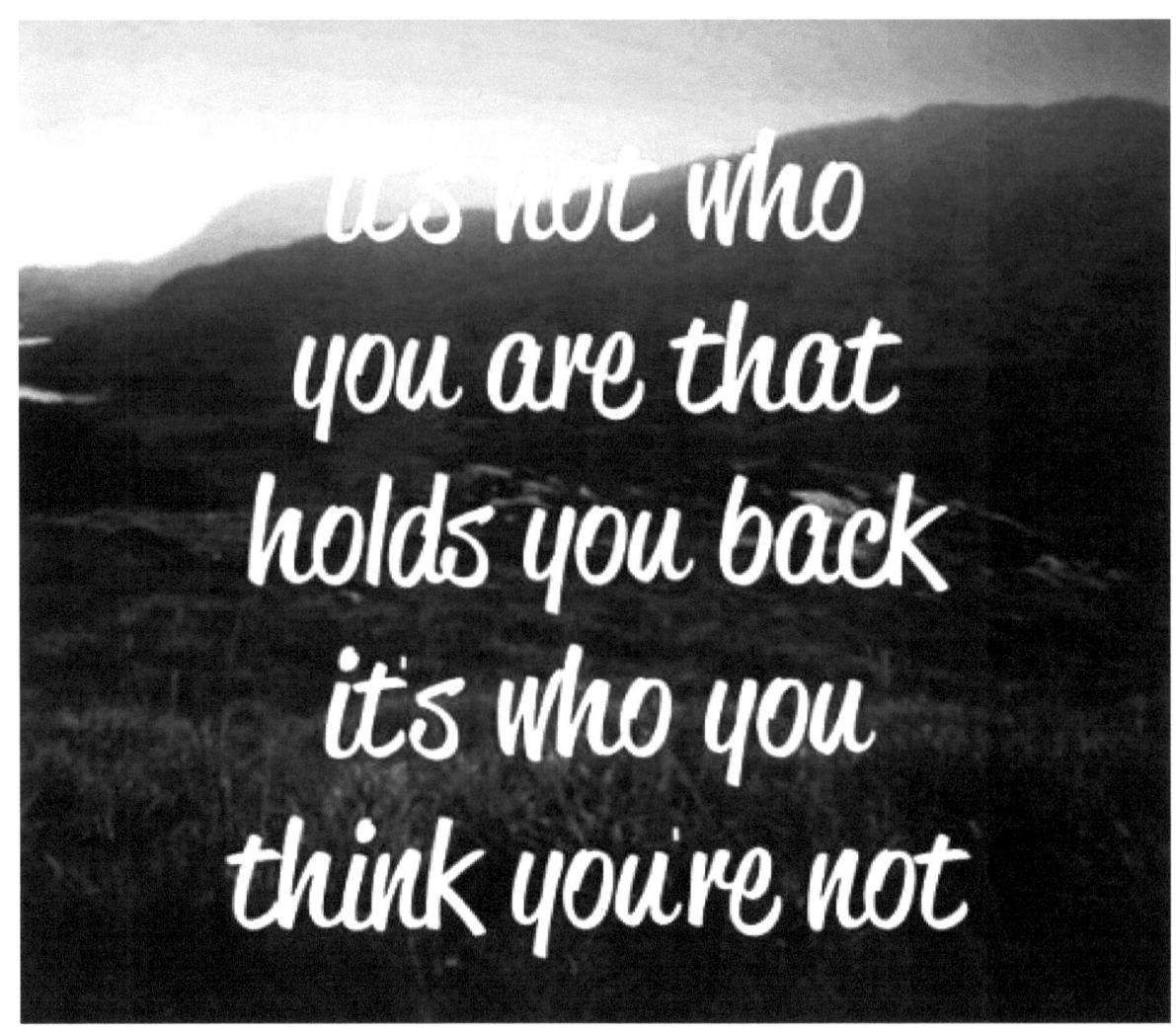

"The Power you hold once you start believing in YOURSELF, will take you beyond your imagination!!"
– KK Smith

Your soul is rooting for you

OPEN UP AND FLY!!!

"IT IS OUR LIGHT, NOT OUR DARKNESS THAT MOST FRIGHTENS US. WE ASK OURSELVES, WHO AM I TO BE BRILLIANT, GORGEOUS, TALENTED, AND FABULOUS? ACTUALLY, WHO ARE YOU NOT TO BE?"

~ Marianne Williamson

I want to say a special Thank you to all that have purchased and read this book. I hope that it gives you the uplifting and motivation you need and more!! Please share with others!!

Also, I want to say Thank you to the contributors of the book, I truly appreciate you!!

May GOD bless you all!

Please checkout Chanique Stewart with www.womenwithambition.me . She is a beautiful, blessed, motivational Life Coach. You can also find more amazing quotes from her on Instagram:@womenwithambition

You can also check out @ThinkGrowProsper on Instagram or purchase their e-book at thinkgrowprosper.org/ebook and

@SingleOrginQuotes is also on Instagram.

Please check out all the other artist noted for more daily inspiration.